The Cleansing KITCHEN

The
Cleansing
KITCHEN

*Feel-good food for
happy and healthy eating*

This edition published by Parragon Books Ltd in 2017
LOVE FOOD is an imprint of Parragon Books Ltd

Parragon Books Ltd
Chartist House
15–17 Trim Street
Bath BA1 1HA, UK
www.parragon.com/lovefood

ISBN 978–1–4748–7467–0

Printed in China

New recipes and introduction by Judith Wills
Cover and new recipe photography by Tony Briscoe

NOTES FOR THE READER

This book uses both metric and imperial measurements. Follow the same units of measurement throughout; do not mix metric and imperial. All spoon measurements are level: teaspoons are assumed to be 5 ml, and tablespoons are assumed to be 15 ml. Unless otherwise stated, milk is assumed to be full fat, eggs and individual fruits and vegetables are medium, pepper is freshly ground black pepper and salt is table salt. A pinch of salt is calculated as $\frac{1}{16}$ of a teaspoon. Unless otherwise stated, all root vegetables should be peeled prior to using.

The times given are an approximate guide only. Preparation times differ according to the techniques used by different people and the cooking times may also vary from those given.

Please note that any ingredients stated as being optional are not included in the nutritional values provided. The nutritional values given are approximate and provided as a guideline only, they do not account for individual cooks, scales and portion sizes. The nutritional values provided are per serving or per item.

While the publisher of the book and the original author(s) of the recipes and other text have made all reasonable efforts to ensure that the information contained in this book is accurate and up to date at the time of publication, anyone reading this book should note the following important points: –
* Medical and pharmaceutical knowledge is constantly changing and the author(s) and the publisher cannot and do not guarantee the accuracy or appropriateness of the contents of this book;
* In any event, this book is not intended to be, and should not be relied upon, as a substitute for appropriate, tailored professional advice. Both the author(s) and the publisher strongly recommend that a doctor or other healthcare professional is consulted before embarking on major dietary changes;
* For the reasons set out above, and to the fullest extent permitted by law, the author(s) and publisher: (i) cannot and do not accept any legal duty of care or responsibility in relation to the accuracy or appropriateness of the contents of this book, even where expressed as 'advice' or using other words to this effect; and (ii) disclaim any liability, loss, damage or risk that may be claimed or incurred as a consequence – directly or indirectly – of the use and/or application of any of the contents of this book.

WHY CLEANSE YOUR DIET?

Most of us know that health and well-being are strongly linked with what we eat – or with what we don't eat. Many minor – and less minor – illnesses and everyday health problems can be prevented, improved or even eliminated by choosing the right diet. For example, two of the major health issues of today, obesity and diabetes type 2, are closely linked with food intake, while heart disease, many types of cancer, arthritis and dementia are all thought to be at least in part diet-related as well.

Research proves that day-to-day energy, vitality, mood and brain function can be improved through food choices as well. Our appearance can also be enhanced by what we eat or choose to avoid. Healthy skin, hair, eyes, gums and nails are largely dependent on a good diet.

Despite all these fantastic potential benefits for choosing an ideal diet, you may still feel that making the necessary changes will be too hard. This is because, for many years now, the idea of cleansing your diet or detoxing has been used to describe a process of rethinking what we eat and drink in order to cleanse our bodies, in particular the liver and digestive system.

Some people might consider the idea of cleansing or detoxing as a drastic, short-term change, usually combined with a very low intake of calories. Indeed the idea of a detox diet can seem extreme and something that you would want to avoid doing for any length of time.

This book sets out to show you a different, more gentle and user-friendly way to cleanse your body and to rethink the way you feel about detoxing. This method is better for the body and provides a more healthy diet, in order to give it the best possible chance to feel healthy, revitalized, toxin-free and running at optimum efficiency.

The recipes in this book are all easy to follow and the ingredients are easy to source, being widely available in most supermarkets or health shops. The results really will delight your taste buds and satisfy your appetite, providing an exciting variety of flavours and textures. Most of the recipes are extremely family-friendly and so all of the family can enjoy the benefits of this clean way of eating, without having to make separate detox meals for one person.

The detox lifestyle that you will enjoy here is something you can – and will want to – stick with every day for the rest of your life. It is not restrictive or boring, but contains meals that you will look forward to making and experimenting with. As the ingredients are often healthy, there is no need to feel hungry either, unlike with other diets.

WHAT IS A CLEANSING DIET?

Our cleansing recipes avoid using certain ingredients that are the most likely to cause adverse reactions within our bodies and are most closely linked to health and well-being problems. The foods we avoid are:

WHEAT AND OTHER GLUTEN-CONTAINING GRAINS

While only a small percentage of people have coeliac disease, a serious allergy to gluten, the number is growing and people who suffer from non-coeliac gluten sensitivity (NCGS) have similar symptoms. Other people show sensitivity to wheat. A diet high in wheat and refined grains has also been linked with obesity and high blood sugar levels.

REFINED SUGAR

Numerous studies across the world have found a link between refined sugar consumption and obesity, diabetes, dental health and cardiovascular disease. The World Health Organization recently recommended a drastic reduction in our refined sugar intake.

DAIRY FOODS

Two thirds of the adult population of the world cannot digest lactose, a component of dairy milk, properly, according to the US National Library of Medicine. Cow's milk consumption has also been linked to acne, some cancers, inflammation and other health problems.

PROCESSED FOODS

Foods that have gone through an intensive manufacturing process tend to contain E numbers and additives, as well as being high in salt, sugar, fats and potential toxins.

ALCOHOL

Long-term or high intake of alcohol can cause high blood pressure, heart disease, strokes, liver disease and digestive problems, as well as depression, insomnia, dementia and many other health issues.

RED MEAT

Consumption of red meat, such as beef, pork and lamb, and processed and smoked meats, is linked with an increased risk of some cancers and heart disease, as well as inflammation and damage to the digestive system. A high animal protein diet may also cause kidney problems.

TOO MUCH SALT

A high salt diet is linked with an increased risk of high blood pressure, as well as with fluid retention, and may make symptoms of several conditions, including asthma and arthritis, worse.

CAFFEINE

Caffeine-rich drinks such as coffee, tea and cola are linked with insomnia, nervousness, panic attacks, irritability, increased heart rate and stomach upsets and also tend to raise blood sugar levels.

WHAT YOU CAN EAT ON A CLEANSING DIET

Our natural recipes will help you to eat a diet that contains all the nutrients you need for health and well-being. You will not be going short on carbohydrates, protein or fats, and the foods featured are bursting with natural health-giving plant chemicals, vitamins, minerals and fibre. The recipes are also packed with foods known to boost your immune system, increase 'friendly' gut bacteria and assist the liver, which is the main detoxifying organ of the body. Here are some of the important food groups in our recipes:

FRUITS AND VEGETABLES

Fruits and vegetables will form a large part of any cleansing or detox diet. They provide healthy carbohydrates, fibre, plant chemicals and vitamin C. Many types of fruit and vegetables, such as beetroot, lemons, the brassica family, apples, celery and artichokes, are also known to support liver function and to promote a healthy gut.

NUTS AND SEEDS

Nuts and seeds are rich in healthy fats and are a great source of non-animal protein, minerals and vitamins. They are extremely versatile ingredients and form an important part of a detox diet. They are also useful for snacking on to stave off hunger.

PULSES

Pulses, such as lentils and dried beans, are one of the best plant sources of protein. They also contain fibre-rich carbohydrates, plant chemicals for health protection, and vitamins and minerals. They are easily added to stews and casseroles to boost the nutritional value of a meal.

WHOLEGRAINS

If you are avoiding wheat, rye, barley and oats in your diet, you can still enjoy a wide range of grains and grain-like plants that are known to be suitable for gluten and wheat-sensitive people. In this book, we have used some of these tasty health-packed grains, such as quinoa, buckwheat and cornmeal.

DAIRY ALTERNATIVES

Foods, such as almond, hazelnut, coconut, rice and soya, are easily digested and ideal to replace standard dairy foods in the diet. They can be made into milks, yogurts, creams and butters and provide easy substitutions for dairy products.

OILY FISH

Oily fish is rich in vital omega-3 fats, which offer health protection in many ways. So it is good to include oily fish, such as salmon, herring, mackerel and sardines, on a detox regime to provide vital fats in your diet.

MAKING GOOD CHOICES

It is important to make good choices when selecting ingredients for your everyday diet. Examples of this are oils and seasonings. For cooking oils, you can choose several types of plant-based oils but there are a few things to bear in mind.

Remember that many plant oils have a low smoking point, which means that if you use them to cook at very high temperatures, their healthy fats can oxidize and become unhealthy. Olive oil – particularly cold–pressed and extra virgin olive oil – has a fairly low smoke point so cook over low or medium heat for as short a time as possible. Rapeseed oil and coconut oil have a higher smoke point and so are more suitable for cooking at higher temperatures.

For salads, all of the plant, seed and nut oils can create fantastic dressings, being rich in healthy fats and vitamin E. Try to use cold–pressed or extra virgin oils in salads as they contain highest levels of health–protective plant chemicals. Olive, rapeseed and hazelnut oil are great sources of monounsaturated fats, while flaxseed oil, hempseed oil, walnut oil and rapeseed oil contain good amounts of omega–3 fats.

To cut down on salt, there are lots of alternative seasonings available to people on a detox diet. It helps to use plenty of other alternative flavourings to provide zest and flavour. Herbs are indispensible – soft herbs, such as basil, parsley, tarragon and coriander leaf, can be used as they are, stirred in or on top of a dish. Other firmer herbs, such as rosemary, bay leaves and thyme, are ideal in cooked dishes.

Fresh and dried spices can be used to enhance almost any dish and all herbs and spices are rich in plant chemicals and antioxidants while some, including cinnamon and turmeric, are liver–supporting and form an important part of any detox plan. Don't forget juices, such as lime, lemon and orange juices, which are great in salad dressings. Many types of vinegar, from sweet balsamic through to sherry, cider and rice vinegars, are ideal for dressings and cooked dishes and some are thought to be digestive aids.

You can add sweetness to detox dishes in a variety of ways. Most fruits – dried, fresh, puréed or chopped – are ideal and they also add nutrients, fibre and flavour. Unrefined sugars, such as coconut palm sugar and molasses, offer a high level of sweetness and flavour. Molasses is rich in iron and other minerals. Syrups can also be a good choice for sweetening – from maple syrup through to date syrup, as well as agave nectar and brown rice syrup. These syrups also have a minimal impact on blood sugars. Raw honey can be another good choice as it has antiseptic qualities and, again, adds flavour and sweetening.

Try to buy organic, raw and unrefined produce whenever you can, if possible, for maximum health benefits on a cleansing detox diet.

A CLEANSING DIET FOR HEALTH

There is much research to show that your health, your well-being and your lifespan can be improved by eating more of the healthy foods that are described on page 11 and fewer of the foods that are described on page 8. In essence, following this food balance is what cleansing or detoxing your diet means. It allows you to give your body, including the detoxing organs the liver, kidneys, skin and lungs, and the lymphatic and digestive systems, the best chance to work optimally and therefore for your body to be healthy, free from disease and functioning as you want it to.

Featured below are the main benefits that people notice when they follow the balanced way of eating that we have described in this book. These benefits are likely to become more obvious and more pronounced over time:

~ Weight loss
~ Reduction in fluid retention
~ Improved digestive function
~ Increased energy
~ Better sleep
~ Better skin
~ Improved mood – less chance of depression and anxiety.

There are important other long–term health benefits too. You may reduce your risk of getting several major diseases, including heart disease, cancers, diabetes type 2, arthritis and dementia, and a cleansing diet can reduce the severity of some of the symptoms. People who have diabetes type 2 may even become free from it.

You can boost the effects of your gentle long–term detox by taking regular, moderate exercise – for example, take a 20–30 minute walk most days, increasing your pace as you become fitter. Exercise has also been shown to help rid the body of harmful chemicals. Some gentle exercise encourages the lungs to work harder (by increasing your heart rate) and it stimulates all of the detoxing organs so that they too work more effectively.

Remember to drink sufficient fluids when following a cleansing diet. Plain water is ideal or juices and smoothies are also good in moderation. Keeping well hydrated will help to ensure that your digestive system, liver and kidneys function well.

F.A.Q. ABOUT DETOX DIETS

Q: WILL I FEEL HUNGRY?

A: No. If you eat and drink regularly and choose a variety of meals and snacks from our recipes you will not be reducing your calories so low that you feel hungry. And, of course, you can always add in extra snacks, such as nuts, seeds, non-dairy yogurt and raw vegetables, if you do feel hungry between meals. Such a diet will be high in fibre and low on the glycaemic index, two important factors in reducing hunger.

Q: CAN I DETOX IF I AM VERY PHYSICALLY ACTIVE?

A: Yes. You simply need to make sure that you eat enough calories so that you have plenty of energy to see you safely through your active lifestyle. Meals and snacks containing good amounts of carbohydrates (check the nutrition panels in this book) are ideal to eat before and after exercise, as well as fruit and nuts for snacking if needed.

Q: WHAT IS THE DIFFERENCE BETWEEN A CLEANSING DIET AND A CRASH DIET?

A: Crash diets are usually very low in calories and tend to focus on a very limited number of foods. Our detox recipes do not require you to do either of these things as we aim for a longer-term change of habits.

Q: IS IT HARD TO FIND THE INGREDIENTS FOR THE RECIPES?

A: No. We have made sure that all the ingredients are widely available in supermarkets or health food stores.

Q: WILL A CLEANSING EATING PLAN BE VERY EXPENSIVE?

A: It certainly does not have to be. While some of the ingredients are more expensive than others, many are low in cost and easily available from a wide variety of sources. You will also save money by avoiding expensive or unnecessary items that are not part of your new diet, such as red meat, alcohol and processed snacks. Shopping wisely and choosing fresh produce that is in season will also help you to save.

Q: IS A CLEASING DIET SAFE TO FOLLOW?

A: Yes, it is very safe. If you follow our guidelines and recipes, you will be choosing a healthy way to eat, which will also give your body's natural 'detoxing' mechanisms, particularly the liver, as much support as possible. It is essential to consult your doctor before starting the diet if you have any special health issues or particular concerns.

BREAKFASTS AND JUICES

Raw carrot, apple and goji bircher muesli	20
Date and chia pudding	22
Spiced quinoa porridge with berries	24
Baked eggs with asparagus	26
Smashed avocado with toasted hemp seeds	28
Spicy black bean and sweetcorn scramble with toasted polenta	30
Kale and banana smoothie	32
Beetroot and chard juice	34
Green tea juice	36
Carrot and cucumber juice	38
Spinach energy booster juice	40
Tantalizing tomato juice	42

RAW CARROT, APPLE AND GOJI BIRCHER MUESLI

Buckwheat grains are soaked overnight for easy digestion and packed with masses of other healthy ingredients to create a delicious, good-for-you version of Swiss bircher muesli.

SERVES: 4

PREP: 15 MINS, PLUS OVERNIGHT SOAKING   COOK: NONE

125 g/4½ oz buckwheat flakes
1 carrot, grated
2 red-skinned apples
150 ml/5 fl oz apple juice
150 ml/5 fl oz almond milk
1½ tbsp dried goji berries
2 tbsp chopped hazelnuts
2 tbsp dried chopped apricots
1½ tbsp shelled pistachio nuts
1 tbsp sunflower seeds

1. Put the buckwheat flakes and carrot in a large bowl. Core, thinly slice and chop one of the apples and add to the bowl. Stir the bowl contents well until thoroughly combined. Stir in the apple juice, almond milk and 1 tablespoon of the goji berries. Cover and leave overnight in the refrigerator.

2. Stir the hazelnuts into the bowl. Core, thinly slice and chop the remaining apple.

3. Divide the muesli between serving dishes and sprinkle the apple, remaining goji berries, apricots, pistachio nuts and sunflower seeds over the muesli. Serve immediately.

MILK ALTERNATIVE
If you prefer a creamier option, you can use all almond milk to soak the flakes instead of using the apple juice.

PER SERVING: 260 KCALS | 7G FAT | 0.7G SAT FAT | 47G CARBS | 18.3G SUGARS | 7.3G FIBRE | 6.7G PROTEIN | TRACE SALT

DATE AND CHIA PUDDING

Chia seeds, when soaked overnight in coconut milk, make a beautifully silky-smooth dish that is high in healthy fats and ideal for an elegant breakfast with little preparation.

SERVES: 2
PREP: 10 MINS, PLUS OVERNIGHT SOAKING   COOK: NONE

3 tbsp chia seeds
225 ml/8 fl oz coconut milk
½ tbsp date syrup
seeds from ½ vanilla pod
3 tbsp coconut soya yogurt
1 large medjool date, chopped
½ orange, sliced
1 tbsp pomegranate seeds

1. Place the chia seeds, coconut milk, date syrup, and vanilla seeds in a large bowl. Stir thoroughly to combine. Tip into a covered container and leave to soak overnight in the refrigerator.

2. When ready to serve, divide the chia mixture into serving bowls. Spread the coconut yogurt over the top of each pudding, then top with the date, orange slices and pomegranate seeds.

3. Serve immediately.

CHEERS FOR CHIA
Chia seeds are rich in omega-3 fatty acids, fibre and minerals and their nutrients are easily absorbed by the body.

PER SERVING: 226 KCALS | 12.6G FAT | 6.6G SAT FAT | 26.3G CARBS | 14.9G SUGARS | 8.4G FIBRE | 5.1G PROTEIN | 0.1G SALT

SPICED QUINOA PORRIDGE WITH BERRIES

High in protein and fibre, quinoa flakes make a perfect start to the day and will keep any hunger pangs at bay until lunchtime.

SERVES: 4
PREP: 5 MINS COOK: 6 MINS

100 g/3½ oz quinoa flakes
1 tbsp ground linseeds
½ tsp sea salt
½ tsp ground cinnamon
¼ tsp ground ginger
¼ tsp ground nutmeg
550 ml/17 fl oz almond milk
1 tbsp agave nectar
2 tbsp goldenberries
3 tbsp dessicated coconut flakes
40 g/1½ oz fresh blueberries
40 g/1½ oz fresh raspberries
40 g/1½ oz fresh blackberries

1. In a large bowl, combine the quinoa flakes, linseeds, salt and spices.

2. Heat the almond milk in a saucepan and add the quinoa flake mixture. Stir and bring to a simmer, then add the agave nectar. Cook, stirring frequently, for about 6 minutes, or until you have a fairly thick porridge and the flakes are soft. Add a little extra milk or water, if you prefer a thinner porridge, and stir in well.

3. Ladle the porridge into serving bowls and top each with a quarter of the goldenberries, coconut flakes and fresh berries. Serve immediately.

GORGEOUS GOLDENBERRIES

Goldenberries are dried physalis – this fruit is also known as Chinese lanterns or cape gooseberries.

PER SERVING: 198 KCALS | 6.1G FAT | 1.8G SAT FAT | 29.8G CARBS | 10.4G SUGARS | 6.1G FIBRE | 4.9G PROTEIN | 0.9G SALT

BAKED EGGS
WITH ASPARAGUS

Protein-rich eggs retain their rightful place on the breakfast table — and pairing them with vitamin- and fibre-rich asparagus provides a healthy, tasty treat.

SERVES: 2
PREP: 10 MINS COOK: 12 MINS

1¼ tbsp extra virgin rapeseed oil
½ tsp paprika
1 garlic clove, crushed
¼ tsp sea salt
¼ tsp pepper
12 asparagus spears, tough ends removed
4 eggs
1 tomato, deseeded and diced
1 tbsp snipped fresh chives

1. Preheat the oven to 190°C/375°F/Gas Mark 5. In a small bowl, combine 1 tablespoon of the oil with all but a pinch of the paprika. Thoroughly stir in the garlic, salt and pepper.

2. Coat the asparagus spears thoroughly in the flavoured oil then place in two shallow gratin dishes. Roast in the preheated oven for 7 minutes, or until nearly tender when pierced with a sharp knife.

3. Crack the eggs evenly over the asparagus and drizzle over any remaining seasoned oil. Return to the oven for 5 minutes, or until the whites are set and the yolks still runny.

4. Serve the eggs and asparagus with the diced tomatoes and chives sprinkled over the top. Drizzle with the remaining rapeseed oil and garnish with the remaining pinch of paprika.

FRESHER THE BETTER
Try to ensure that the eggs you use are very fresh so that the whites do not spread too much across the asparagus when you crack them into the dish.

PER SERVING: 252 KCALS | 18.5G FAT | 3.7G SAT FAT | 7.2G CARBS | 3.4G SUGARS | 3.3G FIBRE | 15.2G PROTEIN | 1.1G SALT

SMASHED AVOCADO WITH TOASTED HEMP SEEDS

The brilliant combination of avocado and hemp seeds gives you a perfect balance of fats and a wide range of plant chemicals.

SERVES: 2
PREP: 5 MINS COOK: 1-2 MINS

2 tbsp raw hemp seeds
2 ripe avocados, roughly chopped
1 tbsp lemon juice
½ tbsp extra virgin olive oil
1 large garlic clove, crushed
½ tsp sea salt
½ tsp pepper
2 x 45 g/1¾ oz slices gluten-free
wholegrain bread, toasted
½ fresh red chilli, deseeded and finely chopped,
to garnish

1. Place a small, non-stick frying pan over a medium heat. Add the hemp seeds and toast them for 1–2 minutes, then set aside in a small dish.

2. Place the avocado in a large bowl. Add the lemon juice, oil, garlic, salt, pepper and 1½ tbsp of the toasted hemp seeds. Stir to combine, then mash to a rough purée.

3. Serve on the wholegrain toast, sprinkled with the remaining hemp seeds and the chopped chilli.

TIME-SAVING TIP
If you want to save a little time at breakfast, you can prepare the avocado mixture the evening before. Just level the surface of the mixture and pour over a thin layer of olive oil to stop the fruit from browning.

PER SERVING: 464 KCALS | 32.3G FAT | 4.1G SAT FAT | 38.8G CARBS | 3G SUGARS | 13.6G FIBRE | 8.8G PROTEIN | 1.8G SALT

SPICY BLACK BEAN AND SWEETCORN SCRAMBLE WITH TOASTED POLENTA

A Mexican-inspired version of scrambled eggs on toast,
this provides a marvellous weekend breakfast or brunch.

SERVES: 2
PREP: 10 MINS, PLUS RESTING   COOK: 20 MINS

70 g/2½ oz fine yellow cornmeal
1 tsp low-salt gluten-free vegetable bouillon powder
1 tbsp nutritional yeast flakes
½ tsp sea salt
1 tbsp extra virgin rapeseed oil, plus 1 tsp for brushing
25 g/1 oz finely chopped red onion
25 g/1 oz finely chopped sweet red pepper
1 small garlic clove, crushed
3 tbsp sweetcorn kernels, cooked and rinsed
3 tbsp black beans, cooked and rinsed
1 tsp sugar-free chilli sauce
4 eggs, beaten

1. Line a 15-cm/6-inch square shallow dish or baking tray with baking paper.

2. Make the polenta at least 2 hours before you want to toast it. Put the cornmeal in a small jug. Bring 375 ml/13 fl oz of water to the boil in a saucepan with the vegetable bouillon powder and when it is fast boiling, gradually pour in the cornmeal, stirring all the time. Continue cooking over a high heat for 3 minutes and stirring until it thickens. Turn the heat down, stir in the nutritional yeast and salt and simmer, stirring frequently, until you have a fairly thick paste.

3. Spoon the cornmeal mixture into the prepared dish or tray. Cover with clingfilm or foil and place in the refrigerator for 2 hours, or until quite firm. Cut into four triangles.

4. Add half of the oil to a small frying pan and place over a medium heat. Cook the onion and pepper for 7 minutes, or until soft. Stir in the garlic, sweetcorn, beans and chilli sauce and cook for a further minute. Set aside and keep warm.

5. Preheat a ridged griddle pan or the grill to medium. Lightly brush the polenta triangles with the 1 teaspoon of oil and grill until turning golden and flecked dark brown. Turn over and grill the other side.

6. In a separate, small frying pan, add the remaining oil and place over a medium heat. Add the eggs and cook, stirring with a spatula or wooden spoon from time to time until lightly scrambled. Gently stir the bean mixture into the eggs and serve with the toasted polenta.

PER SERVING: 427 KCALS | 19.9G FAT | 4G SAT FAT | 43.2G CARBS | 2.4G SUGARS | 3.9G FIBRE | 19G PROTEIN | 2.7G SALT

KALE AND BANANA SMOOTHIE

This creamy smoothie tastes like a naughty treat but is actually very good for you!

SERVES: 1
PREP: 5 MINS COOK: NONE

40 g/1½ oz curly green kale
200 ml/7 fl oz chilled water
1 tsp hemp seeds or hemp seed oil
100 g/3½ oz frozen banana
1 tsp raw cacao powder, plus ⅛ tsp to garnish
¼ vanilla pod, seeds scraped

1. Roughly chop the kale, then add to a blender with the water and blend until smooth.

2. Add the hemp seeds, banana, cacao and vanilla seeds, and blend again until smooth and creamy. Serve immediately, with the raw cacao to garnish.

BANANA BLITZ
To freeze bananas, peel them then freeze them on a tray for 30 minutes, spaced well apart. When frozen, transfer to polythene bags or plastic containers. Use within 3–4 months.

PER SERVING: 133 KCALS | 2.4G FAT | 0.4G SAT FAT | 28.1G CARBS | 13.1G SUGARS | 5.1G FIBRE | 4.3G PROTEIN | TRACE SALT

BEETROOT
AND CHARD JUICE

*This thirst-quenching, nutrient-packed juice
is bursting with vitamins and minerals.*

SERVES: 1
PREP: 5 MINS COOK: NONE

1 beetroot, halved
½ lime
55 g/2 oz red chard
675 g/1 lb 8 oz watermelon,
thickly sliced and peel removed
small handful of ice (optional)

1. Feed the beetroot and lime, then the chard and watermelon through a juicer.

2. Half-fill a glass with ice (if using), then pour in the juice and serve immediately.

BEET IS BEST
Beetroot contains virtually all the vitamins
and minerals needed to give your whole
body a boost.

PER SERVING: 216 KCALS | 1.1G FAT | 0.1G SAT FAT | 53.1G CARBS | 40.2G SUGARS | 5.9G FIBRE | 5.9G PROTEIN | 0.5G SALT

GREEN TEA JUICE

Green tea is packed with antioxidants. Combined with ginseng and wheatgrass, this is a great detoxifying juice that will cleanse you from the inside out.

SERVES: 1
PREP: 5 MINS COOK: NONE

300 ml/10 fl oz green tea
juice of ½ lemon
¼ tsp liquid ginseng
1 tsp pea protein
1 tsp wheatgrass powder
1 tsp maca powder
ice cubes, to serve

1. Whisk the green tea with the lemon juice, ginseng, pea protein, wheatgrass powder and maca powder. Alternatively, you could combine the ingredients in a blender.

2. Serve immediately over ice.

PARTY PUNCH
To cater for a summer party or a garden party with friends, scale up the recipe, chill the punch and pour from a serving jug.

PER SERVING: 62 KCALS | 0.6G FAT | TRACE SAT FAT | 7.6G CARBS | 0.7G SUGARS | 2.6G FIBRE | 6.8G PROTEIN | TRACE SALT

CARROT AND CUCUMBER JUICE

If you don't have a cos lettuce, you can choose iceberg instead.
You can also use Little Gem but you will need two of these.

SERVES: 1
PREP: 5 MINS COOK: NONE

½ cos lettuce
2 tomatoes
2-cm/¾-inch piece of fresh ginger
1 spring onion
1 celery stick, halved
1 carrot, halved
¼ cucumber, plus a slice to garnish (optional)
small handful of ice (optional)

1. Feed the lettuce and tomatoes, then ginger, onion, celery, carrot and cucumber through a juicer.

2. Half-fill a glass with ice (if using), pour in the juice, add the cucumber slice to garnish (if using) and serve immediately.

KNOW YOUR ONIONS
Onions, leeks and garlic are rich in antiviral and antibacterial nutrients that are thought to cleanse the system. They are most potent when eaten raw, but use just a little as they have a strong flavour.

PER SERVING: 144 KCALS | 1.5G FAT | 0.1G SAT FAT | 30.8G CARBS | 14.6G SUGARS | 3G FIBRE | 7.4G PROTEIN | 0.3G SALT

SPINACH ENERGY BOOSTER JUICE

*This is a great energy boosting drink, making it perfect
for breakfast or a mid-morning pick-me-up.*

SERVES: 1
PREP: 5 MINS COOK: NONE

70 g/2¾ oz spinach
2 tsp acai powder
2 tsp manuka honey
1/16 tsp ground cinnamon
250 ml/9 fl oz almond milk
crushed ice, to serve (optional)

1. Place the spinach, acai powder, honey and cinnamon in a blender.

2. Pour over the almond milk and blend until smooth and creamy.

3. Stir well, pour over the crushed ice, if using, and serve immediately.

NUT ALLERGY
If you have a nut allergy, you can replace
the almond milk with coconut or rice milk instead
for another dairy–free alternative.

PER SERVING: 130 KCALS | 6G FAT | 2.2G SAT FAT | 17G CARBS | 12.1G SUGARS | 3G FIBRE | 3.1G PROTEIN | 0.3G SALT

TANTALIZING TOMATO JUICE

*For this drink, pick the best quality tomatoes you can find.
Homegrown or freshly picked ones are perfect, or ones sold on the vine.*

SERVES: 1
PREP: 5 MINS COOK: NONE

2 carrots, halved
1 celery stalk, halved
2.5–cm/1–inch slice of broccoli stem
6 basil leaves, plus a sprig to decorate
4 tomatoes
small handful of ice (optional)

1. Feed the carrots, then the celery, broccoli and the basil, and finally the tomatoes through a juicer.

2. Fill a glass halfway with ice (if using), then pour in the juice. Garnish with the basil sprig and serve immediately.

HOW TO JUICE HERBS
To get the most juice from herbs, sandwich them between firmer fruit or vegetables, so that their weight helps to press down on the leaves as they go through the juicer chute.

PER SERVING: 126 KCALS | 1G FAT | 0.1G SAT FAT | 27.5G CARBS | 15.7G SUGARS | 2G FIBRE | 5.2G PROTEIN | 0.3G SALT

LUNCHES

Lemon chicken courgetti	46
Vietnamese prawn rice rolls	48
Black sesame tofu	50
Chilled green soup	52
Carrot and cashew pâté on crackers	54
South Indian lentil broth	56
Buckwheat noodle salad	58
Energizing rocket soup	60
Baked salmon with sweet potato and cucumber ribbons	62
Baba ghanoush dip with red cabbage salad	64
Puy lentils with roast vegetables	66
Frisée salad with walnut dressing	68
Grilled mackerel with cauliflower couscous	70

LEMON CHICKEN COURGETTI

*If you've never tried creating your own 'spaghetti' from vegetables,
such as courgettes, you'll love how quick and easy it is and how great it tastes.*

SERVES: 4
PREP: 10 MINS COOK: 8 MINS

4 courgettes, 2 green and 2 yellow
2½ tbsp olive oil
2 large chicken breast fillets, cut crossways
into 10 slices
1 tsp crushed coriander seeds
1 tsp crushed cumin seeds
½ tsp sea salt
½ tsp pepper
juice of 1 lemon
2 tbsp toasted pine nuts
3 tbsp fresh coriander leaves

1. Using a spiralizer, the side of a box grater or vegetable peeler, slice the courgettes into spirals or thin ribbons.

2. Add ½ tablespoon of the oil to a non-stick frying pan and place over a high heat. Fry the chicken slices for 1–2 minutes, or until lightly flecked with golden brown, turning once or twice. Turn the heat down to medium and add half of the remaining oil, the seeds, salt, pepper and half of the lemon juice.

3. Cook, stirring occasionally, for 5 minutes, or until the chicken slices are cooked through. Check that the centre of the chicken is no longer pink.

4. Meanwhile, heat the remaining oil in another large frying pan, add the courgette spirals and stir for 1–2 minutes, or until just tender and turning golden. Serve the chicken on the courgetti and scatter over the remaining lemon juice, pine nuts and coriander leaves.

COURGETTE FIBRE
Courgettes are a good source of vitamin C and soluble fibre, which may help to relieve irritable bowel symptoms.

PER SERVING: 250 KCALS | 14.7G FAT | 2G SAT FAT | 5.3G CARBS | 3G SUGARS | 1.6G FIBRE | 24.6G PROTEIN | 0.9G SALT

VIETNAMESE PRAWN RICE ROLLS

Wonderfully light and practically fat-free, these moreish snacks are full of protein-rich shellfish and crunchy raw vegetables.

SERVES: 6
PREP: 40 MINS COOK: NONE

40 g/1½ oz vermicelli rice noodles
150 g/5½ oz chilled, prepared tiger prawns, rinsed
with cold water, drained and thickly sliced
grated zest of 1 lime
10 g/¼ oz fresh mint, leaves torn from stems
10 g/¼ oz fresh coriander, long stems trimmed
55 g/2 oz beansprouts, rinsed and drained
55 g/2 oz carrots, cut into matchstick strips
¼ cucumber, halved lengthways, deseeded
and cut into matchstick strips
½ cos lettuce heart, leaves shredded
6 x 20-cm/8-inch rice spring roll wrappers

DIPPING SAUCE
juice of 1 lime
1 tbsp tamari
1 tbsp light muscovado sugar
1 tsp Thai fish sauce
1 red chilli, halved, deseeded and finely chopped
2 garlic cloves, finely chopped
2.5-cm/1-inch piece fresh ginger,
peeled and finely grated

1. Add the noodles to a shallow dish, cover with just-boiled water, then leave to soften for 5 minutes.

2. Mix the prawns with the lime zest. Arrange the mint, coriander, beansprouts, carrot sticks, cucumber sticks and shredded lettuce in separate piles on a tray. Drain the noodles and tip into a dish.

3. Pour some just-boiled water into a large, shallow round dish then dip one of the rice wrappers into the water. Keep moving in the water for 10–15 seconds until soft and transparent, then lift out, draining well, and place on a chopping board.

4. Arrange a few prawns in a horizontal line in the centre of a rice wrapper, leaving a border of wrapper at either end. Top with some mint leaves and coriander sprigs, then add a few noodles and beansprouts. Add some carrot and cucumber, and a little lettuce. Roll up the bottom third of the rice wrapper over the filling, fold in the sides, then roll up tightly to form a sausage shape. Place on a plate.

5. Repeat with the remaining wrappers until you have 6 rolls.

6. To make the dip, add the lime juice to a small bowl, stir in the tamari, sugar and fish sauce, then add the chopped chilli, garlic and ginger, and stir.

7. Cut each roll in half and serve immediately with individual bowls of the dipping sauce. If planning to serve later, wrap each roll in clingfilm and chill in the refrigerator for up to 8 hours.

PER SERVING: 112 KCALS | 0.4G FAT | TRACE SAT FAT | 22G CARBS | 4.8G SUGARS | 1.4G FIBRE | 4.9G PROTEIN | 1.2G SALT

BLACK SESAME TOFU

Tofu, made from soya bean curd, is a versatile ingredient and works best in flavourful dishes, such as this tasty stir-fry. This makes a brilliant, speedy meal for lunch.

SERVES: 2
PREP: 10 MINS COOK: 15 MINS

1 egg, beaten
1 tbsp tamari
1½ tbsp black sesame seeds
250 g/9 oz firm tofu, cut into bite-sized chunks
70 g/2½ oz rice noodles
2 tbsp sesame oil
150 g/5½ oz small broccoli florets
1 large garlic clove, crushed
½ tbsp lemon juice
1 tsp chilli flakes
½ tsp pepper
1 tsp crushed coriander seeds
1 tsp runny honey
2 spring onions, sliced, to garnish
2 tbsp fresh coriander leaves, to garnish

1. Combine the beaten egg with half of the tamari in a shallow dish. Place the black sesame seeds in a separate shallow dish. Coat the tofu chunks with the egg mixture and then dip each chunk into the sesame seeds.

2. Cook the noodles according to the packet instructions. Drain, cover and set aside.

3. Add half of the sesame oil to a non-stick frying pan and place over a medium-high heat. Stir-fry the broccoli for 2–3 minutes, then add the garlic, lemon juice, chilli, pepper, and coriander seeds. Stir for another minute or two, or until the broccoli is just tender. Stir in the honey, cover the pan and set aside.

4. Heat the remaining oil in another frying pan over a medium heat. Add the tofu chunks and fry them for 3 minutes, turning once or twice. Serve the tofu with the broccoli mixture and noodles and garnish with the sliced spring onions and coriander leaves.

TERRIFIC TOFU
Tofu is cholesterol free and is a good source of protein, iron, calcium and fibre. It is also quick to cook and ideal in stir-fries as it readily picks up the flavours you add to the pan.

PER SERVING: 568 KCALS | 31G FAT | 4.8G SAT FAT | 49.2G CARBS | 5G SUGARS | 7.9G FIBRE | 29.7G PROTEIN | 1.5G SALT

CHILLED GREEN SOUP

This simple yet invigorating soup with refreshing cucumber and plenty of chilled water will cool you down on a hot day.

SERVES: 2
PREP: 10 MINS COOK: NONE

180 g/6¼ oz cucumber
2 celery sticks
2 tbsp chopped fresh parsley,
plus 2 extra sprigs to garnish
2 tbsp chopped fresh mint
2 tbsp chopped fresh coriander
250 ml/9 fl oz chilled water

1. Chop the cucumber and celery and add to a blender with the parsley, mint, coriander and water. Blend until smooth.

2. Serve immediately or chill in the refrigerator and stir just before serving, garnished with parsley.

COOL AS A CUCUMBER
There is some evidence that cucumber can help to build and maintain healthy connective tissue as we age. It is a good source of the mineral silica, which is an essential component of this tissue, as well as of bone and muscle.

PER SERVING: 25 KCALS | 0.2G FAT | TRACE SAT FAT | 4.9G CARBS | 2.3G SUGARS | 1.8G FIBRE | 1.2G PROTEIN | 0.1G SALT

CARROT AND CASHEW PÂTÉ ON CRACKERS

Here is a pâté that is quick to make but has a fresh flavour and a delicious hint of herbs and spices, so it's good enough to serve on a special occasion.

SERVES: 4

PREP: 5 MINS, PLUS SOAKING AND CHILLING   COOK: NONE

140 g/5 oz raw cashew nuts
300 g/10½ oz carrots, chopped
55 g/2 oz light tahini
juice of 1 lemon
2 tsp finely chopped ginger
1 large garlic clove, crushed
½ tsp sea salt
2 tbsp chopped fresh coriander leaves
50 g/1½ oz microsalad leaves, to serve
8 gluten–free mixed seed crackers
(see page 120 or shop–bought), to serve

1. Soak the cashew nuts in a large bowl of cold water for at least 4 hours, or overnight if you have time. Drain thoroughly.

2. Place all of the ingredients, except the fresh coriander leaves, in an electric food processor or blender. Process until you have a smooth mixture.

3. Stir the coriander leaves into the mixture and spoon into 8–cm/3¼–inch round ramekins. Cover with clingfilm and chill for 2 hours before serving.

4. Spread the pâté onto the crackers and serve immediately with the microsalad leaves.

CASHEW CRAVINGS
Cashews are high in energy–promoting iron, the antioxidant mineral zinc and nerve–calming magnesium, while sesame seeds have a range of health benefits, including protection from heart disease.

PER SERVING: 453 KCALS | 34.3G FAT | 5.1G SAT FAT | 28.5G CARBS | 6.4G SUGARS | 9.6G FIBRE | 15.5G PROTEIN | 1.3G SALT

SOUTH INDIAN LENTIL BROTH

This wonderfully warming soup is great for lunch – for a more filling dinner, serve with brown rice.

SERVES: 4
PREP: 10 MINS COOK: 30–35 MINS

100 g/3½ oz pigeon peas (tuvar dal)
600 ml/1 pint cold water
1 tsp ground turmeric
2 tbsp vegetable or groundnut oil
1 tsp black mustard seeds
7 fresh curry leaves
1 tsp cumin seeds
1 fresh green chilli
1 tsp tamarind paste
1 tsp salt

1. Rinse the pigeon peas under cold water, then place in a saucepan with the water, turmeric and 1 tablespoon of oil. Cover and simmer for 25–30 minutes, or until lentils are cooked and tender.

2. Heat the remaining oil in a frying pan over a medium heat. Add the mustard seeds, curry leaves, cumin seeds, chilli and tamarind paste. When the seeds start to pop, remove the pan from the heat and add to the lentil mixture with the salt.

3. Return the broth to the heat for 2–3 minutes. Ladle into warmed bowls and serve immediately.

TASTY TURMERIC

Turmeric comes from a plant native to Indonesia and southern India. The yellow pigment in turmeric has been known to offer protection against inflammatory diseases.

PER SERVING: 163 KCALS | 7.7G FAT | 1.2G SAT FAT | 18.7G CARBS | 1.2G SUGARS | 4.3G FIBRE | 6G PROTEIN | 1.5G SALT

BUCKWHEAT NOODLE SALAD

A Japanese-inspired salad made with just-cooked soba noodles and speckled with nutrient-boosting broccoli and protein-packed edamame beans.

SERVES: 4
PREP: 10 MINS COOK: 10 MINS

150 g/5½ oz soba noodles
200 g/7 oz frozen edamame beans
225 g/8 oz broccoli, cut into
small florets, stems thinly sliced
1 red pepper, halved, deseeded and thinly sliced
1 purple or orange pepper,
halved, deseeded and thinly sliced
115 g/4 oz chestnut mushrooms, thinly sliced
85 g/3 oz ready-to-eat sprouting sunflower seeds

DRESSING
2 tbsp rice wine vinegar
2 tbsp tamari
4 tbsp rice bran oil
4-cm/1½-inch piece of fresh ginger,
peeled and finely grated

1. Put some cold water in the base of a steamer, bring to the boil, then add the noodles and frozen edamame beans and bring back to the boil. Put the broccoli in the top of the steamer, then put it on the steamer base, cover and steam for 3–5 minutes, or until the noodles and vegetables are just tender. Drain and rinse the noodles and edamame beans, then drain again and tip into a salad bowl. Add the broccoli, then leave to cool.

2. To make the dressing, put the vinegar, tamari, oil and ginger in a jam jar, screw on the lid and shake well. Drizzle over the salad and toss gently together.

3. Add the red and purple peppers and mushrooms to the salad and toss again. Spoon into four bowls, then top with the sprouting seeds and serve immediately.

EDAMAME BEANS
Fresh soya beans are a good source of all the essential amino acids, making them an excellent bean to eat if you're following a vegetarian diet. They are also a good source of vitamin K, folate, manganese and fibre.

PER SERVING: 496 KCALS | 28.9G FAT | 4.4G SAT FAT | 45G CARBS | 6.6G SUGARS | 9.2G FIBRE | 17.8G PROTEIN | 1.1G SALT

ENERGIZING ROCKET SOUP

*The mild spice from the rocket and mustard leaves is softened
by the avocado and coconut milk, creating a creamy but healthy soup.*

SERVES: 1
PREP: 10 MINS COOK: NONE

30 g/1 oz rocket,
plus 10 g/ ¼ oz extra leaves to garnish
20 g/¾ oz mustard leaves
200 ml/7 fl oz chilled water
½ avocado, stoned and flesh scooped from skin
125 ml/4 fl oz coconut milk

1. Put the rocket, mustard leaves and water into a blender and blend until smooth.

2. Add the avocado flesh to the blender with the coconut milk and blend until smooth and creamy.

3. Serve immediately or chill in the refrigerator. Stir well just before serving, garnished with a few rocket leaves.

ROCKET ROUSER
Wild rocket leaves are rich in carotenes
and are an excellent source of lutein, which
is good for eye health. The indoles in rocket are
also linked to protection from colon cancer.

PER SERVING: 379 KCALS | 37.9G FAT | 25.2G SAT FAT | 11.9G CARBS | 4.4G SUGARS | 6.1G FIBRE | 5.4G PROTEIN | TRACE SALT

BAKED SALMON WITH SWEET POTATO AND CUCUMBER RIBBONS

A simple and refreshing lunch that is packed with nutrition,
as it contains vitamins C and E as well as essential omega-3 fatty acids.

SERVES: 4
PREP: 15 MINS COOK: 16 MINS

2 sweet potatoes
1½ tbsp extra virgin rapeseed oil
½ tsp sea salt
½ tsp pepper
1 cucumber, topped and tailed
1 tbsp white wine vinegar
1 tsp mild–flavoured runny honey, such as acacia
4 x 125 g/4½ oz thick salmon fillets
2 tsp crushed cumin seeds
1 tbsp chopped fresh dill, to garnish

1. Preheat the oven to 190°C/375°F/Gas Mark 5. Slice the sweet potatoes lengthways into long, thin ribbons using a vegetable peeler, the side of a box grater or a spiralizer. Toss the ribbons in a bowl with half of the oil and half of the salt and pepper then arrange on a baking tray. Place the tray near the top of the preheated oven and cook for 6 minutes. Leave the oven on.

2. Meanwhile, slice the cucumber into long, thin ribbons using a vegetable peeler, the side of a box grater or a spiralizer. Place the ribbons in a bowl. Mix together the vinegar and honey in a small bowl then sprinkle the mixture over the cucumber ribbons and stir gently to combine.

3. Place the salmon fillets on a baking tray, brush with the remaining oil, sprinkle with the crushed cumin seeds and the rest of the salt and pepper and place the tray in the centre of the oven. At the same time, use tongs to turn the sweet potato ribbons over and return them to the oven.

4. Bake for a further 10 minutes, or until the salmon is cooked through and the potato ribbons are tender and turning golden. If the potatoes need another minute or two, remove the salmon from the oven and leave to stand while the potatoes finish cooking.

5. Serve the salmon with the potato ribbons and the dressed cucumber ribbons on the side. Garnish with the chopped dill.

PER SERVING: 340 KCALS | 18.9G FAT | 1.6G SAT FAT | 26.7G CARBS | 7.7G SUGARS | 3.8G FIBRE | 27.4G PROTEIN | 1G SALT

BABA GHANOUSH DIP
WITH RED CABBAGE SALAD

*Grilling aubergines until blackened all over
gives this dip a wonderfully smoky flavour.*

SERVES: 4
PREP: 10 MINS COOK: 20 MINS

2 carrots
350 g/12 oz red cabbage, shredded
55 g/2 oz raisins
125 g/4½ oz bistro salad, a mix of red–stemmed baby
red chard, bull's blood chard and lambs lettuce
juice of 1 orange
½ tsp pepper

DIP
3 aubergines
3 garlic cloves, finely chopped
2 tbsp tahini
3 tbsp hemp oil
pepper (optional)

1. To make the dip, preheat the grill to high and remove the grill rack. Prick both ends of each aubergine with a fork, put them in the grill pan and grill 5 cm/2 inches away from the heat source, turning several times, for 15–20 minutes, or until blackened. Leave to cool.

2. Shave the carrots into long, thin ribbons using a swivel–bladed vegetable peeler, then put them on a serving plate. Add the cabbage, then sprinkle over the raisins and salad leaves. Drizzle with the orange juice and season with the pepper.

3. Cut the aubergines in half and scoop the soft flesh away from the blackened skins using a dessertspoon. Finely chop the flesh, then put it in a bowl. Add the garlic, tahini and hemp oil, season with a little pepper, if using, and mix. Spoon into a serving bowl and nestle in the centre of the salad. Allow diners to spoon the dip over the salad to taste.

RED CABBAGE FOR DETOX
With its intense deep–purple colour,
red cabbage has a strong concentration
of antioxidants–flavonoids that have been
linked to cancer protection.

PER SERVING: 309 KCALS | 8.4G FAT | 0.9G SAT FAT | 43.6G CARBS | 25.6G SUGARS | 13.5G FIBRE | 7G PROTEIN | 0.3G SALT

PUY LENTILS WITH ROAST VEGETABLES

Lentils and whole grains are vital in any detox diet. Rich in complex carbs, fibre, protein, vitamins and minerals, they make a filling base to any meal.

SERVES: 4
PREP: 15 MINS COOK: 30 MINS

2 small red peppers, quartered and deseeded
2 courgettes, thickly sliced
2 red onions, each cut into 8 wedges
400 g/14 oz tomatoes, halved
300 g/10½ oz baby aubergines, halved lengthways
3 stems of fresh thyme, leaves picked
2 garlic cloves, finely chopped
½ tsp pepper
3 tbsp olive oil
225 g/8 oz puy lentils
25 g/1 oz fresh flat-leaf parsley, roughly chopped, to garnish

DRESSING
3 tbsp hemp oil
2 tbsp balsamic vinegar
juice of 1 lemon
pepper (optional)

1. Preheat the oven to 200°C/400°F/Gas Mark 6. Arrange the pepper, skin side up, in a large roasting tin. Add the courgettes, onions, tomatoes and aubergines and arrange in a single layer.

2. Sprinkle the thyme and garlic over the vegetables. with the pepper and drizzle over the olive oil. Roast for 30 minutes, or until the vegetables are softened and browned around the edges.

3. Put the lentils in a saucepan of boiling water. Bring back to the boil, then simmer for 20 minutes, or until just tender. Drain into a sieve, rinse with cold water, then drain again. Transfer to a salad bowl and leave to cool.

4. To make the dressing, put the hemp oil, balsamic vinegar and lemon juice in a jam jar and season with pepper, if using. Screw on the lid and shake well.

5. Drizzle the dressing over the lentils and toss gently together. Peel the skins away from the peppers and cut into slices, then add them to the salad. Add the remaining roast vegetables and any pan juices, then garnish with the parsley and serve.

HOLD THE SALT

On a detox, you should cut right down on salt. Take the salt shaker from the table and gradually cut down on the amount you use in cooking. Add spices, herbs, garlic and vinegars instead.

PER SERVING: 476 KCALS | 15G FAT | 1.8G SAT FAT | 57.2G CARBS | 13.6G SUGARS | 12.3G FIBRE | 17.4G PROTEIN | TRACE SALT

FRISÉE SALAD WITH WALNUT DRESSING

This simple yet flavour-packed salad is lovely and light, with crispy leaves and honey-toasted walnuts.

SERVES: 4
PREP: 10 MINS COOK: 5 MINS, PLUS COOLING

½ frisée lettuce, leaves separated
and torn into bite-sized pieces
1 cos lettuce heart, leaves separated
and torn into bite-sized pieces

DRESSING
55 g/2 oz walnut pieces, larger pieces broken up
3 tbsp olive oil
1 tsp runny honey
1 tbsp white wine vinegar
1 tsp gluten-free Dijon mustard
¼ tsp pepper

1. To make the dressing, put the walnuts in a frying pan, add 1 tablespoon of the oil and cook over a medium heat for 2–3 minutes, or until lightly toasted. Remove from the heat, drizzle over the honey and stir. The heat from the pan will be enough to caramelize the mixture slightly.

2. Add the remaining oil, stir, then leave to cool for 15 minutes so the walnuts flavour the oil. When it is cool, put the vinegar and mustard in a small bowl, season with the pepper and beat together. Stir this into the walnuts and oil.

3. Put the lettuces in a salad bowl. Spoon over the walnut dressing, toss gently together and serve.

WALNUT WONDER
Walnuts contain mostly polyunsaturated fatty acids. They are also rich in protein and fibre, and they provide many of the essential amino acids.

PER SERVING: 224 KCALS | 19.7G FAT | 2.3G SAT FAT | 10.8G CARBS | 3.8G SUGARS | 6.3G FIBRE | 4.9G PROTEIN | 0.1G SALT

GRILLED MACKEREL WITH CAULIFLOWER COUSCOUS

You won't miss standard grain couscous once you've tried the cauliflower version – it really is gorgeous, tasty and light. The herbs and spices give a zesty finish that goes well with oily fish.

SERVES: 4
PREP: 15 MINS COOK: 6 MINS

CAULIFLOWER COUSCOUS

1 cauliflower
1 tbsp extra virgin olive oil
zest and juice of 1 lime
1 red chilli, deseeded and finely chopped
4 spring onions, chopped
1 garlic clove, very finely chopped
15 g/½ oz fresh flat-leaf parsley, chopped
10 g/¼ oz fresh mint leaves, chopped
½ tsp sea salt
½ tsp black pepper

MACKEREL

4 x 125 g/4½ oz skin-on mackerel fillets
1 tbsp extra virgin olive oil
1 tsp sweet smoked paprika
1 lime, quartered

1. Grate the cauliflower into a large bowl (discarding the central core) or cut it into small florets then pulse in a food processor for a few seconds until you have couscous-like 'grains'. Add the oil, lime zest and juice, chilli, spring onions, garlic, herbs, salt and pepper. Mix thoroughly to combine.

2. Line a grill pan with foil and preheat the grill to high. Make three cuts across the skin sides of the fish with a sharp knife and rub in the oil and paprika. Grill for 5 minutes skin-side up, or until crisp, then turn over with a spatula and cook for a further minute.

3. Divide the cauliflower couscous between serving plates and top with the mackerel. Serve immediately with the lime wedges.

MIGHTY MACKEREL

Mackerel is very high in healthy omega-3 fats, with around 2.6g in each 100g – researchers often recommend consuming around 1–2g of omega-3 fats a day.

PER SERVING: 369 KCALS | 24.6G FAT | 5.1G SAT FAT | 11.4G CARBS | 3.7G SUGARS | 3.8G FIBRE | 26.6G PROTEIN | 1.1G SALT

MAINS

Raw vegetable lasagne	74
Steamed mussels in lemon grass broth	76
Creole chicken with coriander parsnip rice	78
Quinoa pizza with cashew cheese	80
Vegetable pho	82
Tamarind turkey with courgette noodles	84
Grilled cauliflower steaks with kale slaw	86
Tofu and miso salad	88
Monkfish and purple sprouting broccoli coconut curry	90
Pea and sprouting seeds buckwheat power bowl	92
Cauliflower and butter bean stew	94
Indonesian gado gado salad	96
Roast fennel and artichoke with caraway dressing	98

RAW VEGETABLE LASAGNE

There are several elements to this gorgeous raw vegan lasagne, but it really is quite easy to put together and is ideal for a dinner party.

SERVES: 2

PREP: 1 HOUR 30 MINS   COOK: NONE

225 g/8 oz courgettes, thinly sliced lengthways
½ tbsp olive oil
2 tsp balsamic vinegar
¼ tsp salt

NUT CHEESE LAYER

100 g/3½ oz shelled weight macadamia nuts
½ small yellow pepper, diced
1 tbsp nutritional yeast flakes
1½ tbsp lemon juice
¼ tsp salt

TOMATO SAUCE

2 tbsp tomato purée
½ tsp garlic purée
¼ tsp smoked paprika
½ tsp salt (optional)

AVOCADO PESTO

40 g/1½ oz pine nuts
1 large ripe avocado, roughly chopped
3 tbsp fresh basil leaves
1 small garlic clove, crushed
juice of ½ lime
¼ tsp salt

2 large tomatoes
30 g/1 oz baby spinach leaves, destalked
2 tsp pine nuts and 2 tsp basil leaves, to garnish

1. To make the courgette layer, place the courgettes in a dish that will hold the slices in one layer. Cover the slices with the oil, vinegar and salt, ensuring that each slice is well covered, then set aside for up to 1 hour to soften and absorb the flavours.

2. To make the cheese layer, pulse all the ingredients in a blender until you have a smooth, light paste.

3. To make the tomato sauce, combine all the ingredients in a small bowl and then add approximately 2 tablespoons of cold water and mix thoroughly. Add a little more water until you have a pouring consistency. Add salt, if using.

4. To make the avocado pesto layer, put the pine nuts in an electric chopper or blender and process for a few seconds, or until chopped but not puréed. Add the avocado chunks, basil leaves, garlic, lime juice and salt and pulse until you have a lightly textured mixture. Slice the tomatoes so that you have six inside slices from each. Discard the outer slices.

5. Layer up the two lasagne directly onto plates. Arrange a quarter of the courgette slices in a rectangle on the centre of each plate. For each plate, top with a quarter of the spinach leaves, then spoon on a quarter of the nut cheese. Add a quarter of the tomato slices and top those with a quarter of the avocado pesto. For each plate, add another quarter of the tomato slices, quarter of the cheese, quarter of the spinach, and quarter of the avocado pesto. Finish by placing the remaining courgette slices on top of each lasagne. Toast the pine nuts in a dry frying pan. Drizzle the sauce over the two lasagne and garnish with toasted pine nuts and basil leaves.

PER SERVING: 799 KCALS | 72.6G FAT | 9.9G SAT FAT | 37.8G CARBS | 14.1G SUGARS | 16.5G FIBRE | 15.1G PROTEIN | 2.3G SALT

STEAMED MUSSELS IN LEMON GRASS BROTH

The clean, refreshing flavour of lemon grass is perfect with the richly flavoured mussels in this filling broth.

SERVES: 4
PREP: 10 MINS COOK: 20 MINS

2 shallots, chopped
2 lemon grass stalks, fibrous outer leaves discarded,
stems bashed with the flat of a knife
4 thin slices galangal or fresh ginger
2 garlic cloves, chopped
1 small tomato, chopped
300 ml/10 fl oz gluten-free fish stock
900 g/2 lb live mussels, scrubbed and debearded
40 g/1½ oz butter
2 tbsp chopped fresh coriander, to garnish
salt and pepper (optional)

1. Put the shallots, lemon grass, galangal, garlic and tomato in a large, covered wok. Pour in the stock, season to taste with salt and pepper, if using, and bring to the boil. Reduce the heat slightly and simmer for 5 minutes.

2. Discard any mussels with broken shells and any that refuse to close when tapped. Tip the mussels into the wok, cover and cook for 5 minutes, shaking the wok occasionally, until the mussel shells have opened. Discard any mussels that remain closed.

3. Drain the mussels in a colander set over a bowl. Strain the liquid using a sieve into a small wok. Simmer over a low heat for a few minutes, then whisk in the butter. Taste and adjust the seasoning, if necessary.

4. Divide the mussels between warmed bowls. Pour over the liquid, garnish with the coriander and serve immediately.

MUSSEL POWER
Mussels are low in saturated fat and high in protein, while also containing some omega-3 essential fats and a wide range of vitamins and minerals in good amounts. They are also low in dietary cholesterol.

PER SERVING: 142 KCALS | 9.8G FAT | 5.7G SAT FAT | 6.5G CARBS | 1.1G SUGARS | 0.6G FIBRE | 7.6G PROTEIN | 1.4G SALT

CREOLE CHICKEN WITH CORIANDER PARSNIP RICE

Creole dishes are full of vegetables and strong on flavour and colour, so are sure to please around the dinner table. This tasty take on Chicken Creole is low in calories but packed with nutrients.

SERVES: 4
PREP: 15 MINS   COOK: 30 MINS

2 tbsp extra virgin rapeseed oil
4 small chicken breast fillets,
each sliced into 3 pieces
1 large onion, sliced
2 celery sticks, finely chopped
1 green pepper, deseeded and thinly sliced
1 yellow pepper, deseeded and thinly sliced
2 garlic cloves, crushed
1 tsp smoked paprika
300 g/10½ oz canned chopped tomatoes
1 tsp sea salt
1 tsp pepper
2 large parsnips, roughly chopped
1 tbsp hemp seeds
4 tbsp fresh coriander leaves,
plus a sprig to garnish

1. Heat half of the oil in a large frying pan over a high heat. Add the sliced chicken pieces and fry for 2 minutes, or until very lightly browned. Remove the chicken pieces from the pan with a slotted spatula and transfer to a plate. Set aside.

2. Add the onion, celery and peppers to the frying pan with half of the remaining oil. Turn the heat down to medium and fry, stirring frequently, for about 10 minutes, or until the vegetables have softened and are just turning golden.

3. Stir in the garlic and paprika and cook for 30 seconds. Add the chopped tomatoes and half of the salt and pepper. Return the chicken to the pan, bring to a simmer and cook for 10 minutes.

4. Meanwhile, add the parsnips to the bowl of a food processor. Process on high until they resemble rice grains then stir in the hemp seeds and the remaining salt and pepper.

5. Heat the remaining oil in a frying pan over a medium heat. Stir in the parsnip rice and stir-fry for 2 minutes, then stir through the coriander leaves. Serve the chicken mixture spooned over the parsnip rice and garnished with the coriander sprig.

PARSNIP POWER
Parsnips are rich in soluble fibre, which can help prevent diabetes and high blood cholesterol.

PER SERVING: 339 KCALS | 12.2G FAT | 1.3G SAT FAT | 25G CARBS | 10.1G SUGARS | 6.6G FIBRE | 32.2G PROTEIN | 1.7G SALT

QUINOA PIZZA
WITH CASHEW CHEESE

Generously topped with Mediterranean vegetables,
this pizza also features a delicious, nutty high-protein quinoa base
and a perfect finishing touch in tangy cashew cheese.

SERVES: 2
PREP: 30 MINS, PLUS OVERNIGHT SOAKING
COOK: 20 MINS

CASHEW CHEESE
70 g/2½ oz raw cashew nuts,
soaked overnight in water
1 small garlic clove, crushed
1 tbsp nutritional yeast flakes
½ tbsp lemon juice

TOPPING
50 g/1¾ oz semi-sun-dried tomatoes
40 g/1½ oz passata
1 garlic clove, crushed
½ tsp salt (optional)
½ red pepper, deseeded and sliced
½ green pepper, deseeded and sliced
1 small red onion, cut into 6 wedges
2 tsp dried mixed herbs
5 pieces grilled artichoke heart in oil, drained
1 tomato, roughly chopped

QUINOA BASE
140 g/5 oz white quinoa (soaked in 500 ml/17 fl oz water
for approximately 8 hours)
½ tsp gluten-free baking powder
½ tsp salt
2½ tbsp olive oil, plus 1 tsp for brushing

1. To make the cashew cheese, drain the cashew nuts and add to an electric food processor or blender with the garlic and 3 tablespoons of water. Process until smooth. Stir in the nutritional yeast flakes and lemon juice and process for a few more seconds. For the pizza, you want a 'dropping consistency' texture, not quite as firm as hummus, so add a little extra water if necessary and blend again. Spoon the cheese out and set aside.

2. Preheat the oven to 190°C/375°F/Gas Mark 5. Line a 23-cm/9-inch shallow cake tin with baking paper and grease the paper with 1 teaspoon of oil.

3. To make a tomato paste, blend the sun-dried tomatoes with the passata and garlic. Add salt, if using, and stir in a little water to get a spreading consistency if necessary.

4. To make the quinoa base, drain the water from the quinoa and put into a blender with the baking powder, salt, 60 ml/2 fl oz of water and 2 tablespoons of the olive oil. Blend until you have a thick, creamy batter. Pour into the prepared cake tin and shape into a round. Bake in the preheated oven for 15 minutes, or until the top is golden. Remove from the pan and transfer to a wire rack to cool.

5. Meanwhile, toss the peppers, onion and mixed herbs with the remaining half a tablespoon of oil and roast on a baking tray in the preheated oven for 10–15 minutes, or until softened and turning lightly golden. Remove from the heat and set aside. Spread the tomato paste over the pizza base, leaving the edges clear. Arrange the peppers, onion, artichoke pieces and chopped tomato on the pizza and then drop dollops of the cashew cheese over the top. Return to the oven for 5 minutes, or until the vegetables are hot and the cashew cheese is tinged golden and set.

PER SERVING: 759 KCALS | 44G FAT | 6.8G SAT FAT | 76.2G CARBS | 10.7G SUGARS | 14.1G FIBRE | 21.4G PROTEIN | 2.6G SALT

VEGETABLE PHO

*This wonderful soup is laden with vegetables and noodles,
making it a flavour-packed and filling choice for dinner.*

SERVES: 4
PREP: 10 MINS COOK: 30 MINS

1.5 litres/2½ pints gluten-free reduced-salt
vegetable stock
2 tbsp tamari
2 garlic cloves, thinly sliced
2.5-cm/1-inch piece ginger, peeled and thinly sliced
1 cinnamon stick
1 bay leaf
1 carrot, cut into thin batons
1 small fennel bulb, thinly sliced
150 g/5½ oz vermicelli rice noodles
85 g/3 oz button mushrooms, sliced
115 g/4 oz beansprouts
4 spring onions, thinly sliced diagonally
3 tbsp chopped fresh coriander
fresh basil leaves, chopped red chillies, lime wedges
and tamari, to serve (optional)

1. Place the stock in a large pan with the tamari, garlic, ginger, cinnamon and bay leaf. Bring to the boil, reduce the heat, cover and simmer for about 20 minutes.

2. Add the carrot and fennel and simmer for 1 minute. Add the noodles and simmer for a further 4 minutes.

3. Add the mushrooms, beansprouts and spring onions and return to the boil.

4. Ladle into warmed soup bowls and sprinkle with the coriander. Remove and discard the bay leaf and cinnamon. Serve immediately with basil leaves, chillies, lime wedges and tamari, if using.

BRILLIANT BEANSPROUTS
Beansprouts are ideal to lose weight as they are very low in calories and high in fibre. They are also a good source of vitamin B.

PER SERVING: 205 KCALS | 1.6G FAT | 0.8G SAT FAT | 42.3G CARBS | 5.8G SUGARS | 3.7G FIBRE | 5.8G PROTEIN | 3.6G SALT

TAMARIND TURKEY WITH COURGETTE NOODLES

Detoxing doesn't mean losing the flavour in your food, as this delicious Thai dish will prove. This recipe is rich with health-giving galangal, garlic and chilli.

SERVES: 4
PREP: 15 MINS, PLUS STANDING   COOK: 10 MINS

500 g/1 lb 2 oz turkey breast, diced
1½ tbsp tamari
3 courgettes
1½ tbsp groundnut oil
85 g/3 oz small okra
2.5–cm/1–inch piece fresh galangal or ginger, peeled and grated
3 garlic cloves, crushed
1 large red chilli, finely chopped
1 lemon grass stalk, bashed
2 tbsp rice wine

TAMARIND SAUCE
1 tbsp tamarind paste
100 ml/3½ fl oz gluten–free chicken stock
2 tsp Thai fish sauce
1 tbsp raw palm sugar
1 tsp cornflour

1. Toss the turkey pieces with 1 tablespoon of the tamari to coat. Leave to marinate for five minutes.

2. Meanwhile, make the tamarind sauce by combining all the ingredients thoroughly in a small bowl. Slice the courgettes into thin ribbons, using a spiralizer, the side of a box grater or vegetable peeler.

3. Add half of the oil to a large frying pan and place over a medium–high heat. Add the coated turkey pieces and stir–fry for 3 minutes, or until cooked through. Remove the turkey with a slotted spoon to a warmed plate. Turn the heat down to medium.

4. Add the okra to the pan with the remaining oil and stir–fry for 2 minutes, stirring from time to time. Add the galangal, garlic, chilli, lemon grass, rice wine and remaining tamari and stir for a further 2 minutes. Return the turkey pieces to the pan and add the tamarind sauce. Stir well to combine and simmer for 3 minutes. Add a little extra chicken stock or water if the sauce gets too thick.

5. While the sauce is simmering, steam the courgette noodles over a saucepan of boiling water for 30 seconds to soften and warm. Remove the lemon grass stalk from the turkey mixture and serve immediately, with the noodles on the side.

PER SERVING: 270 KCALS | 8G FAT | 1.4G SAT FAT | 15.4G CARBS | 7.7G SUGARS | 2.3G FIBRE | 32.2G PROTEIN | 1.5G SALT

GRILLED CAULIFLOWER STEAKS WITH KALE SLAW

Once you have tried grilled cauliflower steaks, you will never want to eat it any other way – they really are delicious, especially served with vitamin-rich kale slaw.

SERVES: 4

PREP: 20 MINS, PLUS STANDING   COOK: 15 MINS

KALE SLAW
125 g/4½ oz tender kale leaves, shredded
2 carrots, grated
1 small red onion, thinly sliced
2 tbsp extra virgin rapeseed oil
1 tsp Dijon mustard
½ tbsp cider vinegar
2 tsp maple syrup
sea salt and pepper (optional)
1 tbsp pumpkin seeds
1 tbsp sunflower seeds

CAULIFLOWER STEAKS
2 heads of cauliflower
3 tbsp extra virgin rapeseed oil
juice of ½ lime
1 tsp sweet paprika
1 large garlic clove, crushed
½ tsp sea salt
½ tsp pepper

1. In a serving bowl, combine the kale, carrot and onion. In a small bowl, thoroughly mix together the oil, mustard, vinegar, maple syrup and salt and pepper, if using, and stir into the slaw. Cover and set aside to rest for up to 1 hour. Before serving, sprinkle the seeds over the slaw.

2. Preheat the grill to medium–hot. Meanwhile, remove the leaves from the cauliflower and cut the stalk across the base so it will sit firmly on your chopping board. Using a very sharp knife, cut vertically down about 5 cm/ 2 inches through the first cauliflower. Remove the florets that fall and repeat on the other side so you are left with the firm central piece of the vegetable. Now slice through the cauliflower and stalk to produce 'steaks' that are around 2–2.5 cm/¾–1 inch thick. You should get two steaks from each cauliflower.

3. Cover the rack of a large grill pan with aluminium foil and place the steaks on top. Combine the oil, lime juice, paprika, garlic, salt and pepper in a small bowl and brush the steaks all over with this mixture. Grill the steaks about 5 cm/2 inches from the heat source for 8 minutes, or until the steaks are slightly browned.

4. Turn the steaks over carefully with a large metal spatula and brush again with any remaining oil mixture and the juices which should have collected on the foil. Grill for a further 6 minutes or until the steaks are well coloured and just tender when pierced with a sharp knife. Serve immediately with the kale slaw.

PER SERVING: 296 KCALS | 21.1G FAT | 1.9G SAT FAT | 24.5G CARBS | 10.1G SUGARS | 8.1G FIBRE | 8.1G PROTEIN | 1G SALT

TOFU AND MISO SALAD

Protein-rich tofu cooked in a tamari, miso and garlic glaze and served with a crispy, crunchy asparagus and beansprout salad – super healthy and super lovely!

SERVES: 4
PREP: 15 MINS COOK: 10 MINS

400 g/14 oz firm tofu, drained
and cut into 1–cm/½–inch slices
1 tbsp sesame seeds
85 g/3 oz mangetout, thinly sliced
115 g/4 oz ready–to–eat beansprouts
150 g/5½ oz asparagus,
trimmed and cut into long, thin slices
1 courgette, cut into matchsticks
1 Little Gem lettuce,
leaves separated and cut into long slices
25 g/1 oz fresh coriander, roughly chopped
85 g/3 oz mixed ready–to–eat sprouting seeds, such as
alfalfa and radish sprouts

DRESSING

3 tbsp rice wine vinegar
2 tbsp tamari
3 tbsp sunflower oil
1 tbsp sweet white miso
2 garlic cloves

1. To make the dressing, put the vinegar and tamari in a jam jar, then add the oil, miso and garlic. Screw on the lid and shake well.

2. Preheat the grill to high and line the grill pan with foil. Put the tofu on the foil in a single layer. Mark criss–cross lines over each slice using a knife, then sprinkle with the sesame seeds. Spoon over half the dressing, then grill for 8–10 minutes, turning once, until browned.

3. Put the mangetout, beansprouts, asparagus, courgette and lettuce on a platter. Pour over the remaining dressing and toss gently together. Sprinkle over the coriander and sprouts, then top with the hot tofu. Drizzle with any pan juices and serve immediately.

MISO MAGIC
Miso is associated with good gut health because it feeds the beneficial probiotic bacteria present in the body. This supports the absorption of nutrients to keep you feeling healthy.

PER SERVING: 316 KCALS | 20.9G FAT | 2.5G SAT FAT | 16G CARBS | 6.3G SUGARS | 6.2G FIBRE | 22G PROTEIN | 1.4G SALT

MONKFISH AND PURPLE SPROUTING BROCCOLI COCONUT CURRY

*Fish, coconut and spices were simply made for each other,
as you'll know when you try this quick and simple curry for supper.*

SERVES: 4
PREP: 15 MINS COOK: 20 MINS

1 large onion, chopped
2 tsp fish sauce
juice of ½ lime
2 red chillies, 1 destalked and 1 chopped
1 green chilli, destalked
2 tsp crushed coriander seeds
2 tsp crushed cumin seeds
2.5-cm/1-inch piece fresh ginger, chopped
3 garlic cloves, roughly chopped
½ stalk lemon grass
1½ tbsp groundnut oil
5 curry leaves
300 ml/10 fl oz full-fat coconut milk
350 g/12 oz purple sprouting broccoli,
each spear cut in two
500 g/1 lb 2 oz monkfish fillet, cubed

1. Add the onion, fish sauce, lime juice, destalked chillies, seeds, ginger, garlic, lemon grass and half of the oil to the bowl of a blender or food processor and process until you have a paste. Tip the mixture into a frying pan and cook over a medium heat for 2 minutes. Stir in the curry leaves and coconut milk and simmer for 10 more minutes.

2. Meanwhile, add the remaining oil to another frying pan and place over a high heat. Stir-fry the broccoli for 2 minutes, or until just tender. Set aside.

3. Add the monkfish cubes to the curry pan and bring back to a simmer. Cook for 2 minutes, then add the broccoli spears to the pan and continue cooking for a further minute. Serve the curry with the remaining chopped chilli sprinkled over the top.

BOUNTIFUL BROCCOLI
Purple sprouting broccoli is high in the plant chemical sulforaphane, thought to help prevent cancer, as well as being rich in vitamin C, iron and fibre.

PER SERVING: 346 KCALS | 21.5G FAT | 12.8G SAT FAT | 17.3G CARBS | 6.8G SUGARS | 4G FIBRE | 22.8G PROTEIN | 0.2G SALT

PEA AND SPROUTING SEEDS BUCKWHEAT POWER BOWL

Sprouted seeds and pulses make a wonderful addition to a healthy salad at any time of year, while buckwheat adds fibre and a superb nutty flavour.

SERVES: 4
PREP: 10 MINS, PLUS COOLING   COOK: 20 MINS

4 carrots, cut into quarters lengthways
2½ tbsp extra virgin rapeseed oil
1½ tbsp maple syrup
100 g/3½ oz ready-roasted buckwheat groats
250 g/9 oz mixed sprouted seeds (such as aduki beans, alfalfa, radish and lentil)
¼ cucumber, diced
2 celery sticks, diced
1 red-skinned apple, diced
4 spring onions, diced
60 g/2¼ oz cooked small peas
juice of 1 orange
juice of ½ lemon
½ tsp sea salt
½ tsp pepper
30 g/1 oz pea shoots

1. Preheat the oven to 190°C/375°F/Gas Mark 5.

2. Toss the carrots in ½ tablespoon of the oil and in ½ tablespoon of the maple syrup. Roast in the preheated oven for 20 minutes, or until golden and just tender. Leave to cool.

3. Meanwhile, pour the groats into 175 ml/6 fl oz of boiling water in a large saucepan. Stir and bring to the boil, then reduce to a simmer, put a lid on and cook for 10 minutes, or until the groats are cooked. Turn the heat off and let the pan stand on the heat for a few minutes with the lid on, then tip into a serving bowl and leave to cool.

4. Mix the cooled groats with the sprouted seeds, cucumber, celery, apple, spring onions and peas.

5. Combine the remaining rapeseed oil and maple syrup with the orange and lemon juices and salt and pepper in a small bowl. Stir this dressing into the buckwheat mixture. Top with the roasted carrots and pea shoots, then serve in individual bowls.

SUPER SPROUTS

Seed sprouts and beansprouts contain digestive enzymes – most are rich in antioxidants and are a great source of vitamin C.

PER SERVING: 300 KCALS | 10.1G FAT | 0.8G SAT FAT | 49.3G CARBS | 15.8G SUGARS | 10.5G FIBRE | 9G PROTEIN | 0.9G SALT

CAULIFLOWER AND BUTTER BEAN STEW

This is a hearty and colourful one-pot dish that needs no accompanying carbs as the butter beans contain a good balance of both protein and starch.

SERVES: 4
PREP: 10 MINS COOK: 35 MINS

2 tbsp olive oil
2 large red onions, sliced
2 carrots, cut into 2-cm/¾-inch dice
2 celery sticks, cut into 2-cm/¾-inch dice
3 garlic cloves, crushed
400 g/14 oz canned plum tomatoes in juice
250 ml/9 fl oz gluten-free vegetable stock
1 tbsp sun-dried tomato purée
½ tbsp dried mixed herbs
½ tsp pepper
salt (optional)
800 g/1 lb 12 oz canned butter beans, drained and rinsed
1 head cauliflower, divided into florets
1 tsp sweet paprika

1. Add the oil to a large lidded saucepan and place over a medium-hot heat. Add the onions, carrots and celery and cook for 5 minutes, or until lightly coloured, stirring from time to time. Stir in the garlic and cook for a minute.

2. Add the canned tomatoes, roughly crushing any whole ones against the sides of the pan, and their juice. Stir in the stock, tomato purée, herbs, pepper and salt, if using. Bring to a simmer, reduce the heat to low and place the lid on. Cook for 20 minutes, or until the vegetables are all tender.

3. Stir in the butter beans and cook for a further 5 minutes. Place the cauliflower florets on top of the stew, put the lid back on and simmer for 5 minutes more, or until the cauliflower is just tender when the stalks are pierced with a sharp knife.

4. Serve the stew immediately, garnished with the sweet paprika.

ROMANESCO RULES

You can also make this stew with romanesco if cauliflower is unavailable. Romanesco is a pretty, pale-green type of brassica that is closely related both to broccoli and cauliflower and has similar nutritional benefits.

PER SERVING: 301 KCALS | 9.8G FAT | 1.6G SAT FAT | 39.2G CARBS | 11.3G SUGARS | 12.9G FIBRE | 13G PROTEIN | 0.8G SALT

INDONESIAN GADO GADO SALAD

Tossing raw cauliflower and broccoli with crunchy beansprouts and cucumber and coating them with an Indonesian dressing turns everyday ingredients into something special.

SERVES: 4
PREP: 10 MINS COOK: 5 MINS, PLUS COOLING

250 g/9 oz cauliflower,
cored and cut into small florets
115 g/4 oz broccoli, destemmed
and cut into small florets
115 g/4 oz Savoy cabbage, shredded
150 g/5½ oz ready-to-eat beansprouts
300 g/10½ oz cucumber, peeled, halved lengthways,
deseeded and thickly sliced
1 red pepper, halved,
deseeded and finely chopped

DRESSING
2 tbsp groundnut oil
85 g/3 oz unsalted peanuts, finely chopped
2 garlic cloves, finely chopped
2 tbsp tamari
juice of 2 limes
½ red chilli, deseeded and finely chopped

1. Put the cauliflower, broccoli, cabbage, beansprouts, cucumber and red pepper in a salad bowl and toss together gently.

2. To make the dressing, heat 1 tablespoon of the oil in a frying pan over a medium heat. Add the peanuts and garlic and stir-fry for 2–3 minutes, or until lightly browned. Remove from the heat and stir in the tamari, lime juice, chilli and remaining oil. Leave to cool.

3. When ready to eat, spoon the dressing over the salad and toss together gently. Spoon into four bowls, then serve immediately.

BEANSPROUT BONANZA
Beansprouts are low in calories and can be added to salads and Asian dishes in place of rice or noodles.

PER SERVING: 259 KCALS | 17.8G FAT | 2.6G SAT FAT | 20.4G CARBS | 8.2G SUGARS | 6.6G FIBRE | 10.8G PROTEIN | 1.2G SALT

ROAST FENNEL AND ARTICHOKE WITH CARAWAY DRESSING

An aromatic warm salad ideal for keeping hunger at bay as, although the dish is low in calories, its high fibre content will keep hunger pangs away for several hours.

SERVES: 4
PREP: 10 MINS COOK: 25 MINS

2 large fennel bulbs
1 large sweet red pepper, cut into 12 slices
280 g/10 oz artichoke hearts in olive oil, drained and 2 tbsp of the oil reserved
½ tsp sea salt
½ tsp pepper
1 tbsp white wine vinegar
½ tbsp caraway seeds, lightly crushed
1 tsp runny honey
1 tsp sweet paprika

1. Trim the fennel bulbs of any leaves and reserve these. Slice the fennel into thick slices crossways. Preheat the oven to 190°C/375°F/Gas Mark 5.

2. Brush the fennel and pepper slices with ½ tablespoon of the reserved artichoke oil. Season with a pinch of the sea salt and pepper and roast in the preheated oven for 25 minutes, or until browned (the peppers may need to come out before the fennel). Turn over halfway through.

3. Meanwhile, to make a dressing, combine the remaining 1½ tablespoon of artichoke heart oil with the wine vinegar, caraway seeds, honey, half of the paprika and the remaining salt and pepper. Cut the artichoke hearts in half if they are not already cut.

4. Arrange the fennel and pepper slices on serving dishes with the artichokes. Drizzle over the dressing and serve garnished with the reserved fennel leaves and the remaining paprika.

FANTASTIC FENNEL
Fennel contains several valuable plant chemicals, including rutin, quercetin and kaempferol that have strong antioxidant effects, as well as the anti-inflammatory anethole.

PER SERVING: 128 KCALS | 5.5G FAT | 1.1G SAT FAT | 20.9G CARBS | 8.8G SUGARS | 9.1G FIBRE | 3.3G PROTEIN | 1.6G SALT

DESSERTS AND SNACKS

POACHED RHUBARB
WITH EDIBLE FLOWERS

*There is no need to add sugar to this pretty rhubarb dessert
as the addition of elderflowers provides its own sweetness.*

SERVES: 4
PREP: 10 MINS COOK: 6 MINS

500 g/1 lb 2 oz tender red rhubarb
juice of ½ lemon
1¼ tbsp acacia or other mild honey
flowers from 3 elderflower heads, rinsed
2 tbsp edible flowers such as elderflowers, lavender
flowers and violet flowers or pink rose petals, to serve

1. Cut the rhubarb stalks into 7 cm/2¾ inch pieces and arrange in a large, lidded frying pan in one layer.

2. Combine the lemon juice, honey, 100 ml/3½ fl oz of hot water and the elderflowers from the three heads in a large heatproof bowl. Pour this mixture over the rhubarb and bring to a simmer over a medium–low heat. Put the lid on and simmer for 3 minutes then turn the rhubarb pieces over and simmer for a further 2 minutes, or until the rhubarb is just tender when pierced with a sharp knife. Using a slotted spoon, transfer the fruit to serving bowls.

3. Stir the liquid to reduce to a syrupy consistency and pass through a sieve to remove the cooked elderflower petals. Spoon the syrup over the rhubarb and decorate with elder, lavender, or violet flowers or rose petals to serve.

RHUBARB RULES
Rhubarb is very low in calories and is a well-known laxative, as well as being a good source of calcium and vitamin C.

PER SERVING: 50 KCALS | 0.2G FAT | 0.1G SAT FAT | 12G CARBS | 7.2G SUGARS | 2.5G FIBRE | 1.2G PROTEIN | TRACE SALT

CACAO, CHILLI AND AVOCADO MOUSSE WITH CINNAMON BERRIES

Here's an unusual dessert that you definitely do not have to feel guilty for enjoying – it is full of healthy ingredients and sweetened with agave nectar rather than sugar.

SERVES: 4

PREP: 4¼ HOURS COOK: NONE

2 ripe avocados, halved and stoned
60 g/2¼ oz cacao powder
4 tbsp agave nectar
seeds from ½ vanilla pod
½ tsp chilli powder
50 ml/1¾ fl oz full-fat canned coconut milk
40 g/1½ oz wild or small strawberries
40 g/1½ oz fresh raspberries
½ tsp ground cinnamon

1. Scoop the avocado flesh into a large bowl and mash lightly with fork. Stir in the cacao powder, agave nectar, vanilla seeds and chilli powder. Blend thoroughly with a hand blender until the mixture is thick and smooth. Stir in the coconut milk and blend again.

2. Spoon the avocado mixture into ramekins or small, stemmed glasses. Cover with clingfilm and chill for at least 4 hours.

3. Decorate the avocado mousses evenly with the berries and sprinkle the cinnamon over each dish. Serve immediately.

CACAO RICHNESS
Cacao is rich in antioxidants including flavonoids and catechins – its antioxidant level is higher even than green and black tea, and cacao is also packed with fibre.

PER SERVING: 249 KCALS | 15.8G FAT | 5.1G SAT FAT | 32.9G CARBS | 17G SUGARS | 11.7G FIBRE | 4.9G PROTEIN | TRACE SALT

CHILLED MELON BREEZE SMOOTHIE BOWL

This smoothie bowl will chill you out and cool you down on a hot summer's day. This would also work as a starter or breakfast dish.

SERVES: 1
PREP: 10 MINS COOK: NONE

300 g/10½ oz green melon, peeled and deseeded
250 g/9 oz cucumber
4 tbsp chopped fresh mint, plus a sprig to garnish
200 ml/7 fl oz chilled coconut water

1. Chop the melon and cucumber and place in a blender or food processor.

2. Add the mint, pour over the coconut water and blend until smooth and creamy.

3. Serve immediately or chill in the refrigerator. Stir just before serving, garnished with a sprig of mint.

MELON MAGIC
A melon contains 92 per cent water, which keeps the kidneys working well. All melons are rich in vitamin B6, potassium and soluble fibre.

PER SERVING: 194 KCALS | 1.3G FAT | 0.5G SAT FAT | 44G CARBS | 33.8G SUGARS | 7.4G FIBRE | 5.4G PROTEIN | 0.6G SALT

COCONUT MILK AND STRAWBERRY ICE CREAM

Everyone loves ice cream but it can be loaded with lots of processed sugar.
This version is made with just three wholesome ingredients.

SERVES: 6
PREP: 25 MINS FREEZE: 6 HOURS

450 g/1 lb strawberries, hulled and halved
400 ml/14 fl oz canned full-fat coconut milk
85 g/3 oz clear honey
crushed hazelnuts, to serve (optional)

1. Purée the strawberries in a food processor or liquidizer, then press through a sieve set over a mixing bowl to remove the seeds.

2. Add the coconut milk and honey to the strawberry purée and whisk together.

3. Pour the mixture into a large roasting tin to a depth of 2 cm/³/₄ inch, cover the top of the tin with clingfilm, then freeze for about 2 hours until just set.

4. Scoop back into the food processor or liquidizer and blitz again until smooth, to break down the ice crystals. Pour into a plastic container or 900-g/2-lb loaf tin lined with non-stick baking paper. Place the lid on the plastic container or fold the paper over the ice cream in the loaf tin. Return to the freezer for 3–4 hours, or until firm enough to scoop.

5. Serve immediately or leave in the freezer overnight or until needed. Thaw at room temperature for 15 minutes to soften slightly, then scoop into individual dishes and top with crushed hazelnuts to serve, if using.

STRAWBERRY SUNSHINE
Natural sugars found in the strawberries are absorbed more slowly than those from processed sugars. Strawberries are also an excellent source of vitamin C, manganese and fibre.

PER SERVING: 198 KCALS | 14.4G FAT | 12.6G SAT FAT | 19.3G CARBS | 16.9G SUGARS | 1.5G FIBRE | 1.9G PROTEIN | TRACE SALT

RAW TAHINI CARAMEL SQUARES

*Rich in nuts, cacao and fruit, these truly delicious squares
are great for a healthy dessert or snack.*

MAKES: 16 SQUARES
PREP: 20 MINS, PLUS SOAKING AND CHILLING   COOK: NONE

BASE
40 g/1½ oz semi-dried apples
200 g/7 oz stoned medjool dates
100 g/3½ oz almonds
1 tsp coconut oil
¼ tsp sea salt

CARAMEL
100 g/3½ oz raw cashew nuts
115 g/4 oz stoned medjool dates
4 tbsp coconut oil
2 tbsp light tahini
3 tbsp maple syrup

CHOCOLATE TOPPING
4 tbsp coconut oil
4 tbsp maple syrup
2 tsp date syrup
4 tbsp raw cacao powder
½ tsp vanilla pod seeds

1. Line a 15-cm/6-inch square tin with baking paper, making sure the paper overhangs the edges by 5 cm/2 inches.

2. To make the base, soak the apple pieces in water for 5 minutes then drain and add to a food processor with the remaining base ingredients. Pulse until the dates and nuts are finely chopped and the mixture is fairly sticky. Spoon the mixture into the base of the prepared tin and press down evenly to cover the base. Place in the freezer to chill for at least 15 minutes.

3. To make the caramel, pulse the nuts and dates in a food processor until you have a fairly smooth mixture. Add the oil, tahini and maple syrup and process again to a smooth paste. If necessary, to make a paste of dropping consistency, add 1–2 tablespoons of water and process again. Smooth the caramel on top of the base in the tin and return to the freezer for 1 hour.

4. To make the chocolate topping, heat the oil and syrups in a small saucepan over a medium-low heat and stir in the cacao powder and vanilla seeds. Keep stirring until you have a glossy sauce. Pour this over the cold caramel and return to the freezer for 1 hour, or until the topping is firm.

5. Remove the mixture from the tin by gripping the overhanging paper. Place on a chopping board and cut into 16 squares with a sharp knife. Serve or store in an airtight container in the refrigerator for up to 7 days.

PER SQUARE: 232 KCALS | 14G FAT | 7.1G SAT FAT | 27.7G CARBS | 21.4G SUGARS | 3.3G FIBRE | 3.5G PROTEIN | 0.1G SALT

COCONUT, CACAO AND HAZELNUT TRUFFLES

These small treats are just bursting with a nutritious mix of vital minerals, vitamins, protein and raw ingredients.

MAKES: 20 TRUFFLES
PREP: 25 MINS COOK: NONE

85 g/3 oz unblanched hazelnuts
55 g/2 oz cacao nibs, plus 1 tbsp for coating
6 dried soft figs, roughly chopped
25 g/1 oz desiccated coconut,
plus 2 tbsp for coating
1 tbsp maple syrup
finely grated rind and juice of ½ small orange

1. Add the hazelnuts and the 55 g/2 oz cacao nibs to a food processor and process until very finely chopped.

2. Add the figs, the 25 g/1 oz coconut, maple syrup and orange rind and juice to the processor and process until finely chopped and the mixture has come together in a ball.

3. Scoop the mixture out of the food processor, then cut into 20 even-sized pieces. Roll into small balls in your hands.

4. Finely chop the extra cacao nibs, then mix with the extra coconut on a sheet of non-stick baking paper on a plate. Roll the truffles, one at a time, in the cacao and coconut mixture, then arrange in a small plastic container. Store in the refrigerator for up to 3 days.

RAW CACAO
Unlike cocoa powder, which is made by roasting cacao at high temperatures, raw cacao is cold-pressed to retain more minerals and antioxidants.

PER TRUFFLE: 79 KCALS | 5.5G FAT | 2.4G SAT FAT | 6.3G CARBS | 4.8G SUGARS | 1.7G FIBRE | 1.4G PROTEIN | TRACE SALT

RAW CHOCOLATE, CHERRY AND ALMOND FUDGE BITES

These little cherry-filled bites are very easy and quick to make
— they also contain no added sugar, good-for-you cacao and make an ideal gift too!

MAKES: 35 PIECES
PREP: 10 MINS, PLUS CHILLING   COOK: NONE

100 g/3½ oz unsweetened almond butter
5 tbsp coconut oil
65 g/2¼ oz raw cacao powder
6 tbsp runny honey
¼ tsp sea salt
seeds from ½ vanilla pod
65 g/2¼ oz dried cherries

1. Blend the almond butter and coconut oil in a food processor for a few seconds to combine. Add the cacao powder and blend again.

2. Stir in the honey, salt and vanilla seeds and blend again. Stir in the dried cherries. Do not blend again once the cherries have gone in.

3. Line a shallow tin or tray that is approximately 13 x 10 cm/ 5 x 4 inches with baking paper, allowing the paper to overhang the edges by at least 5 cm/2 inches. Spoon the mixture into the tin and level the surface. Place the mixture in the freezer for about an hour, or until firm.

4. Remove the fudge from the tin by gripping the overhanging paper. Place on a chopping board and, using a sharp knife, cut into five slices lengthways. Then cut each slice into seven squares. Serve or store in an airtight container in the refrigerator.

RING THE CHANGES
For a variation, try the same recipe but use cashew butter instead of the almond butter and chopped dried goldenberries instead of the cherries.

PER PIECE: 55 KCALS | 3.8G FAT | 1.9G SAT FAT | 5.9G CARBS | 3.9G SUGARS | 1.1G FIBRE | 1G PROTEIN | TRACE SALT

RAW DATE AND COCONUT BARS

These chunky, nutty bars get the most out of the raw ingredients. Perfect to keep you energized at work all afternoon long.

MAKES: 12 BARS
PREP: 15 MINS, PLUS CHILLING COOK: NONE

400 g/14 oz medjool dates, halved and stoned
60 g/2¼ oz unblanched almonds
60 g/2¼ oz cashew nut pieces
35 g/1¼ oz chia seeds
2 tbsp maca
seeds from 1 vanilla pod
20 g/¾ oz desiccated coconut
55 g/2 oz unblanched hazelnuts, very roughly chopped
25 g/1 oz pecan nuts, broken in half

1. Add the dates, almonds and cashew pieces to a food processor and process until finely chopped.

2. Add the chia seeds, maca and vanilla seeds, and process until the mixture binds together in a rough ball.

3. Tear off two sheets of non-stick baking paper, put one on the work surface and sprinkle with half the coconut. Put the date ball on top then press into a roughly-shaped rectangle with your fingertips. Cover with the second sheet of paper and roll out to a 30 x 20-cm/10 x 8-inch rectangle. Lift off the top piece of paper, sprinkle with the remaining coconut, the hazelnuts and pecan nuts, then re-cover with the paper and briefly roll with a rolling pin to press the nuts into the date mixture.

4. Loosen the top paper, then transfer the date mixture, still on the base paper, to a tray and chill for 3 hours or overnight, until firm.

5. Remove the top paper, cut the date mixture into 12 pieces, peel off the base paper then pack into a plastic container, layering with pieces of baking paper to keep them separate. Store in the refrigerator for up to 3 days.

DATE DARLINGS
Dates are high in fibre, and are a good source of potassium, calcium, iron, phosphorus and magnesium. They are thought to help with intestinal problems.

PER BAR: 224 KCALS | 11G FAT | 2G SAT FAT | 31.6G CARBS | 23.1G SUGARS | 5.4G FIBRE | 4.2G PROTEIN | TRACE SALT

ROAST SPICY EDAMAME AND CRANBERRIES

Frozen edamame or young soya beans make a healthy, protein-packed snack and their high levels of fibre keep you feeling fuller for longer.

SERVES: 4
PREP: 15 MINS, PLUS COOLING COOK: 15 MINS

350 g/12 oz frozen edamame beans
5-cm/2-inch piece fresh ginger,
peeled and finely grated
1 tsp Sichuan peppercorns, roughly crushed
1 tbsp tamari
1 tbsp olive oil
3 star anise
40 g/1¼ oz dried cranberries

1. Preheat the oven to 180°C/350°F/Gas Mark 4. Place the beans in a roasting tin, then sprinkle over the ginger and peppercorns, drizzle with tamari and oil, and mix together.

2. Tuck the star anise in amongst the beans, then roast, uncovered, in the preheated oven for 15 minutes.

3. Stir in the cranberries and leave to cool. Spoon into a small jar and eat within 12 hours.

EDAMAME ENERGY
Edamame beans are very versatile and pack a much bigger nutritional punch than frozen peas.

PER SERVING: 182 KCALS | 9.2G FAT | 1.1G SAT FAT | 12.7G CARBS | 7.4G SUGARS | 4.4G FIBRE | 11.2G PROTEIN | 0.5G SALT

MIXED SEED CRACKERS

If you've never made your own crackers before, you can't go wrong with these crunchy treats, made with lots of nutritious seeds and no grain at all.

MAKES: 30 CRACKERS
PREP: 10 MINS, PLUS SOAKING AND COOLING
COOK: 1 HOUR 20 MINS

85 g/3 oz chia seeds
85 g/3 oz golden linseeds
85 g/3 oz pumpkin seeds
85 g/3 oz sunflower seeds
2 tbsp ground linseed with berries
1 tbsp sesame seeds
1 tsp sea salt
2 tsp nutritional yeast flakes
½ tsp dried rosemary
½ tsp dried thyme

1. Put the chia seeds and golden linseeds in a large bowl. Tip in 250 ml/9 fl oz of cold water, stir and set aside for 15 minutes. Preheat the oven to 140°C/275°F/Gas Mark 1.

2. Stir in all of the other ingredients and mix well to combine. Line a baking tray that is approximately 28 x 38 cm/11 x 15 inches with baking paper. Tip the cracker mixture onto the baking paper and spread the mixture out evenly across the whole of the tray – you can use your clean fingers or the back of a large spoon to do this.

3. When the mixture is spread evenly, make four evenly spaced lengthways scores into the top half of the mix only. Make five evenly spaced crossways scores so that you have an outline for 30 rectangular crackers. Place the baking tray in the centre of the preheated oven and bake for 45 minutes.

4. Take the tray out and turn the cracker sheet over using two large flat spatulas. (If this proves difficult, cut the cracker sheet into two down one of the pre–made scores, using a large sharp knife, before turning). Return the tray to the oven for a further 35 minutes.

5. Turn the cracker sheet out onto a wooden board (a glass or metal surface will tend to make the crackers break when you're cutting them) and, while still warm, cut into 30 crackers through the score marks. Place on a wire rack to cool for at least 30 minutes then serve or store in an airtight container.

PER CRACKER: 66 KCALS | 5.3G FAT | 0.6G SAT FAT | 3.1G CARBS | 0.2G SUGARS | 2.3G FIBRE | 2.7G PROTEIN | 0.2G SALT

ROAST KALE CHIPS

*Kale's flavour becomes wonderfully intense when the leaves are roasted.
These chips are perfect on their own or sprinkled over soup.*

SERVES: 4
PREP: 20 MINS COOK: 10–12 MINS

250 g/9 oz kale
2 tbsp olive oil
½ tsp sugar
½ tsp sea salt
2 tbsp toasted flaked almonds, to garnish

1. Preheat the oven to 150°C/300°F/Gas Mark 2. Remove the thick stems and central rib from the kale (leaving about 125 g/4½ oz trimmed leaves). Rinse and dry very thoroughly with kitchen paper. Tear into bite–sized pieces and place in a bowl with the oil and sugar, then toss well.

2. Spread about half of the leaves in a single layer in a large roasting tin, spaced well apart. Sprinkle with half of the salt and roast on the bottom rack of the preheated oven for 4 minutes.

3. Stir the leaves, then turn the tray so the back is at the front. Roast for a further 1–2 minutes, or until the leaves are crisp and very slightly browned at the edges. Repeat with the remaining leaves and salt. Sprinkle the kale chips with the flaked almonds and serve immediately. These are best eaten on the day they are made.

KALE KARMA
Kale boasts lots of calcium, vitamins C and B-group, and beta-carotene. It also provides high levels of iron, making this a great vegetable for vegetarians.

PER SERVING: 119 KCALS | 9.7G FAT | 1.1G SAT FAT | 6.8G CARBS | 2.1G SUGARS | 2.7G FIBRE | 3.6G PROTEIN | 0.8G SALT

FIBRE-RICH FRUIT AND NUT TRAIL MIX

Trail mix must be an all-time favourite snack, and this recipe is brimming with energy-boosting and fibre-rich fruit, nuts and seeds.

SERVES: 12
PREP: 10 MINS COOK: NONE

85 g/3 oz chopped ready-to-eat dried apricots
85 g/3 oz dried cranberries
85 g/3 oz roasted cashew nuts
85 g/3 oz shelled hazelnuts
85 g/3 oz shelled Brazil nuts, halved
85 g/3 oz flaked almonds
4 tbsp toasted pumpkin seeds
4 tbsp sunflower seeds
4 tbsp toasted pine nuts

1. Place all the ingredients in an airtight container, close the lid and shake several times.

2. Shake the container before each opening, then re-seal. This mix will stay fresh for up to 2 weeks if tightly sealed.

CASHEW CRAZY

Cashew nuts have a lower fat content than most nuts, and most of their fat is unsaturated fatty acids. They also have a high antioxidant content.

PER SERVING: 267 KCALS | 21.2G FAT | 2.8G SAT FAT | 17.1G CARBS | 9.8G SUGARS | 3.6G FIBRE | 7.2G PROTEIN | TRACE SALT

INDEX